CAREERS WITH

COUNTY AND STATE POLICE

CHOOSING A CAREER SHOULD BE inspiring and fun. What do you like to do? What do you want to get out of your career? Money? Fame? Responsibility? How about deep satisfaction at doing your duty? Serving others? Being a part of something larger than yourself? Those are good goals, too.

Nobody ever said that being a police officer is an easy way to earn a living. The hours can be long and inconvenient, some people will never appreciate what you do, and sometimes the work is dangerous. But policing is also a noble and necessary profession, and the rewards are numerous.

Big-city police departments get most of the glory in movies and television, but state and county police departments are what hold the criminal justice system together. Arrangements vary from state to state, but most county and state police departments provide security to state and county prisons and jails, and to state and county courts. They also patrol the unincorporated areas between incorporated cities. Many also staff and equip high-cost assets like crime labs and police academies, and make them available to municipal police departments too small to maintain their own. State and county police departments are also often the lead agencies on cooperative projects like anti-gang task and drug enforcement task forces undertaken in cooperation with the Federal Drug Enforcement Agency or Federal Bureau of Investigation. State and county police departments (county police departments are usually known as sheriff's departments and are led by a county sheriff elected by the residents of the county) may not get much pop-culture glory, but they can provide a very wide range of career opportunities to dedicated professionals.

WHAT YOU CAN DO NOW

YOU CAN START PREPARING FOR YOUR career in policing right now. Many state and county police departments sponsor Law Enforcement Explorers programs that give young people an inside view of the work of policing. Law Enforcement Explorers is a program sponsored by Learning for Life, a subsidiary of the Boy Scouts of America. The program organizes groups of young people who want to explore careers in policing and pairs them up with police departments. Explorers generally wear their own uniforms – not actual police uniforms, which would be illegal – and work alongside police officers handling the routine responsibilities that police deal with every day. Explorers also take on community-service projects in conjunction with police, like assisting officers with school visits. Participating in an Explorer program comes with no obligation, and Explorers are not allowed to participate in dangerous activities. If your state or county department offers an Explorer program you should check it out.

Many departments also sponsor citizens' police academies. Less formal than the Explorers program, typical citizens' police academies meet for a few hours once or twice a week for two to three months. The format is very much like taking a class. Citizens meet at the police department – or the shooting range, driving skills training center, or even the county morgue – to learn about policing from sworn police officers. For the officers, citizens' police academies are a pleasant way to interact with the people they serve. For the citizens, the academies offer a valuable glimpse into a profession that is often misunderstood by the general public.

There is no easier, faster way to learn about any profession than by reading the periodicals and journals devoted to it. Stories, editorials and even advertisements will give you a broader understanding of the field. Some of the many journals devoted to policing include *Police, Police and Security News* and *Police Chief*. There are also many academic journals devoted to policing, including the *Journal of Law Enforcement* and the *Journal of Policing and Criminal Psychology*.

HISTORY OF THE CAREER

LAW ENFORCEMENT IS ONE OF THE fundamental responsibilities of government. What we call "civilization" is in large part the product of a legal system that helps people live with one another by spelling out expectations for their behavior in advance, and being clear about what will happen when somebody crosses the line. Enforcement of these expectations – laws – is what allows civilization to function smoothly.

This was not always the case. The earliest modern societies left criminal law in the hands of the people. In ancient Greece and Rome, for example, the government devoted itself primarily to military matters. Although soldiers spent most of their time on the battlefield it was not unusual for them to be called upon to quell major domestic unrest. Petty crime was usually dealt with by ordinary people. When a person committed a crime and was caught, justice was served on the spot. A general consensus determined appropriate punishments for various crimes, including murder. Government officials were only called in to make determinations in especially troublesome or high-profile cases.

County sheriffs have a long history, predating the founding of the United States by many centuries. Throughout human history most people lived their entire lives within a few square miles. Roads were poor and horses were the only practical means of long-distance travel. For regular folks the most important unit of government was the county. They may have been English or French or American, but such national seats of authority were so distant as to be almost irrelevant. People lived and worked in counties.

In English common law, the county sheriff was the king's representative to the people. The sheriff enforced the king's laws, collected taxes, and ran the court and the jail. English common law provided the basis for American law centuries later, when early settlers needed basic law enforcement in their new counties. The key difference was that American sheriffs enforced state law, not the king's law. The other responsibilities remained essentially the same. County sheriffs were the most powerful authority in the new nation. This idea was extended to new territories as the country expanded westward. Sheriffs figure so prominently in Western lore because they were often the only government officials for thousands of square miles.

State police departments are a distinctly American phenomenon. Many countries have regional police departments but most report directly to a national authority. The United States is among relatively few countries in which small administrative subdivisions – states – can make most of their own laws and enforce them. All 50 states maintain their own state police departments. Some have different names, like the California Highway Patrol, while others have fairly limited powers, like Hawaii's Department of Public Safety, which generally plays a much smaller role in law enforcement than the county sheriff's departments that serve each island.

Modern county and state police departments serve to fill the geographic gaps between cities, and provide services that would not be practical for small departments to handle on their own. State police departments often run police academies. They also operate first-rate crime labs, and play the primary role in conducting investigations that include multiple jurisdictions. State police departments also patrol state capitols, provide bodyguards for governors and other high state officials, and patrol state highways.

County sheriff's departments fulfill many of the same functions at a more local level. Municipal police departments take the lead in patrolling incorporated cities, but most of the United States is unincorporated territory. County sheriff's departments patrol the wide-open spaces between the cities. They typically maintain county jails and provide patrols and bailiffs for county courthouses. They also serve court summonses and often provide patrol services to incorporated cities too small to maintain their own police departments.

WHERE YOU WILL WORK

EVERY SQUARE INCH OF THE UNITED States is under the jurisdiction of at least one police department, and probably several. If you pursue a career in county or state policing you should be able to work anywhere you want.

Most state and county police activity takes place in small towns and rural areas. The arrangement varies from state to state, but generally, county and state police are responsible for patrolling the areas in-between cities that have their own police departments. Geographically, this includes the overwhelming majority of the country. Demographically, it usually means the places where there are the fewest people. State and county police may have a presence in big cities if they play a large role in running state prisons or county jails located there, and they have to make regular appearances at courthouses located in big cities. Most of the time, however, county and state police are on patrol outside the cities in unincorporated areas.

County and state police departments always have a presence in state capitals and county seats. County and state police departments report to state legislatures and county boards in the same way that the military reports to the federal government in Washington. Some county seats are very large cities. Chicago, for example, is the seat of Cook County, Illinois. Relatively little of Cook County is unincorporated, so the Cook County Sheriff's Police Department has only a small number of deputies on patrol. Mostly, the department provides cooperative services for smaller departments in Cook County, such as crime labs, investigations, and police training. The sheriff's office also includes the Court Services Division and the Department of Corrections, both of which are very large and are based mostly in Chicago.

In some parts of the country, county and state police are the only police. Many small towns cannot afford to maintain a police department of their own so they negotiate contracts with county or state departments to patrol their territory. Interestingly, sociologists have discovered that cities with populations of 600 or less generally do not require regular patrols because everybody knows everybody else and has a stake in their well-being. A city of 1,000 to 2,000 residents may have an arrangement with the county sheriff's office to provide as few as eight hours of patrol each week, just to remind anyone wanting to make trouble that somebody is paying attention.

DESCRIPTION OF WORK DUTIES

ALL COUNTY SHERIFF'S DEPARTMENTS and state police departments are unique institutions. Their basic mission may be similar, but each department has different priorities and different ways of achieving them. Job titles and functions will not be exactly the same from one department to the next. All of the jobs listed here are typically performed by county sheriff's deputies or state troopers. Uniformed personnel are usually deputies or troopers first, and then enter specialized career paths like corrections or patrol. Some officers stay on the same path for their entire career, while others move around and maximize their experience.

Patrol Officer

Patrol officers are what most people envision when they think of police officers. Patrol officers are the hardy souls who spend hours upon hours in patrol cars or on foot, circulating through their assigned beats and keeping an eye out for anything amiss. Most importantly, patrol officers "show the flag" when they drive through a beat, reminding the law-abiding that they are being protected and the law-breaking that they are being watched. This is the reason why many police departments allow their officers to drive patrol cars home at night. A police car parked in plain sight is a powerful deterrent.

County patrol officers are usually responsible for patrolling the unincorporated areas in-between incorporated cities. In urban and suburban counties there may not be very much unincorporated territory, but in most of the United States, counties are almost all unincorporated territory. Look at a map of counties in rural areas and you will see the tiny dots of small towns surrounded by the wide-open spaces of unincorporated territory. Deputy sheriffs have jurisdiction over these spaces, providing basic police patrol services to the people who live in them. Sheriff's deputies also often patrol small towns too small to have their own police department.

State troopers on patrol generally patrol state highways. They usually have jurisdiction throughout their state but spend most of their time patrolling highways and the areas immediately around them. Traffic enforcement is obviously a large part of their job but they are also often the only uniformed presence in the gas stations and small restaurants along state routes. This is especially true of patrol officers assigned to state turnpikes that are closed off to cross traffic. Because they have jurisdiction throughout their state, state troopers on patrol also respond to emergency calls in their districts and assist county and municipal police when needed.

Investigator

Known as detectives in city police departments, state and county investigators are troopers or deputies assigned to investigative functions. They may take the lead in investigating crimes within unincorporated areas or in areas for which they have special responsibility, like state capital districts. They may also assist small police departments with investigations.

State and county investigators are perhaps the best example of the critical role that state and county departments play in assisting smaller departments to solve crimes. Crime labs equipped with the latest scientific equipment are expensive to maintain. Most states and counties have cooperative agreements with their small departments to have access to the experts and facilities operated by the state or county.

State and county investigators often take the lead in complex investigations in small cities. Small departments often lack the expertise to deal with complex cases and have to turn over the day-to-day operations of investigations to state or county investigators with the necessary experience. There was a time when police departments of all sizes zealously protected their turf and did whatever they could to keep larger departments out of their work. Unfortunately, many small departments with small staffs and limited resources botched investigations, inadvertently destroying evidence and making it very difficult for prosecutors to pursue cases. Cooperative agreements are the norm today.

Corrections Officer

Corrections officers may or may not be deputy sheriffs. The distinction depends upon the jurisdiction. In some counties, for example, all corrections officers are sheriff's deputies. In others, corrections officers are on a completely different career path and are not sheriff's deputies even though they wear uniforms and work for the county sheriff. Some counties where corrections officers are also deputies, allow deputies to move back and forth between corrections and patrol during their careers, while others require deputies to choose a path and stick to it. State corrections departments are almost always separate from state police departments and do not use state troopers at all.

County corrections officers are responsible for running county jails. In most states, county jails are responsible for holding suspects awaiting hearings or court proceedings at the county courthouse. County jails may also hold convicts sentenced to relatively short sentences of a year or less. County corrections officers process people who have been arrested. They catalogue their belongings, issue prison uniforms and assign them to cells. They also guard facilities.

Some counties make a distinction between corrections officers and court-services officers. Court-services officers escort suspects to court proceedings and provide security to courthouses and individual courtrooms.

Instructor

Training is a vital part of any police agency. Like the military, police departments have to be prepared at all times. They need the best equipment. They are subject to changing laws and expectations. They need to stay physically fit and spend many hours on the shooting range. Many state troopers and county sheriff's deputies spend a few years as an instructor during their careers.

This is especially true of state troopers assigned to state police academies. State police academies do not train only state police. State police academies train most new police officers in all 50 states. They also offer follow-on training and advanced courses. Only the largest cities maintain their own police academies. In Illinois, for example, only

Chicago runs its own police academy. Police from all other cities in Illinois attend the Illinois State Police Academy in Springfield.

A typical police academy program for new officers takes about six months and is similar to military boot camp. Recruits spend their days exercising and studying. Some academies are residential while others allow recruits to come and go at the end of the day.

State troopers who serve as instructors are usually experienced veterans who take pride in the opportunity to pass along their wisdom to the up-and-coming generation.

County Sheriff

Most county sheriffs are elected officials, and may or may not be career law enforcement officers. Most sheriffs are police officers – because voters tend to think, not unreasonably, that current or former police officers will make good sheriffs – but some are attorneys, prosecutors, or career politicians.

Sheriffs are the chief executive officers of their departments. They are responsible for manning, training and equipping their departments, running the county jail and court-services divisions, and any other responsibilities assigned to them by their county. They usually report to the county board chair in the same way that military leaders report to the president, or that local police chiefs report to their mayor.

County sheriffs are leaders and managers. Many county sheriffs, especially in large departments, have graduate degrees and pursue additional credentials at institutions like Harvard University and Northwestern University, both of which offer advanced academic programs for senior law enforcement personnel. If you want to become a county sheriff someday you should start burnishing your academic credentials and your political skills.

State Police Chief

State police chiefs, who often have the title director, are appointed by governors to run state police departments. They are almost always career police officers and are usually chosen from among senior leadership at the state police department or from a large department in the state. Sometimes governors will look outside the state to appoint a police chief, especially if they need somebody to shake up the department and make unpopular decisions.

Like county sheriffs, state police chiefs are the chief executive officers of their departments. They are ultimately in charge of everything in the state police department. They also represent the department in dealings with their state legislature, which controls their funding. They may also be called upon to testify in legislative hearings in order to provide recommendations on changes to state law.

Special Duty

There are many categories of special duty within county and state policing. Fish and game departments may be separate from state police departments, or specialized departments within the larger department. State colleges and universities often maintain their own police departments. State and county departments with coastlines, lakes or large rivers often maintain maritime units.

State and county departments also often assign deputies or troopers to cooperative task forces with large city departments or federal departments like the United States Marshalls Service or the FBI. Such assignments typically last   three to five years, during which time the deputy or trooper may report to work in a federal or municipal department office. Such joint assignments almost always go to top performers.

OFFICERS TELL THEIR OWN STORIES

I Am a County Sheriff's Department Investigator

"A few years ago there was a horrible crime committed at a fast-food place in a city in the county where I work. It was in a small town, and the officers there don't have much experience with violent crimes. When they responded to the crime scene they failed to take the necessary steps to secure evidence, like taping off the area so nobody else could get into it, and leaving everything in place until detectives could arrive. They did not preserve evidence, which made it very hard to solve the crime.

In response, my county sheriff and all of the local police chiefs in the county got together and hammered out a cooperative arrangement that enabled local departments to call in county investigators to handle major crimes. For too long local departments tried to solve all of their own cases, sometimes with disastrous results. Now we work together on the complex cases, and that serves everybody better.

I always knew that I wanted to be a cop. After high school I served for five years in the Army as a military police officer. I spent a lot of time standing guard duty at the base gates. I started to study for a bachelor's degree in law enforcement while I was still in the service and then finished it after I got out. I was hired by my department fairly quickly based on my military experience, bachelor's degree and high test score. A degree wasn't required by my department, but there's no doubt that it put me at the top of the list.

I spent the first decade of my career on patrol duty. You can't be an investigator until you've spent some time on the street. That's the only way to meet the people and see the crime scenes and start to get a feel for why people sometimes do the crazy things that they do.

Investigating is an art and science like no other. We have amazing scientific tools at our disposal to help us to solve crimes, but human intuition is still the primary tool in our kit. After you've seen enough crimes you start to put two and two together pretty quickly. This is a job for someone who is detail oriented and who can stay focused and think creatively at the same time."

I Am a State Highway Patrol Trooper

"Sometimes it's hard to say that I really like my job. I've seen things that nobody wants to see and dealt with people who were so irrational I couldn't wait to lock them up. Somebody has to do this job   and there's great pride to be taken in doing it well.

I spend most of my time out on the road. Mostly, I see to traffic enforcement on state highways. You'd be amazed at what people think they can get away with when they're in the middle of nowhere. I've pulled people over for driving at well over 100 miles per hour. Some of these knuckleheads were driving sports cars that we could never catch in our patrol cars, and they ask me how I caught them. I have to remind them that nobody can outrun a radio. I never get tired of that line.

I earned an associate degree in law enforcement after high school. My department requires at least two years of college in order to be able to take the academy entrance exam. I learned the basics of criminal law enforcement in school, which prepared me well for the police academy. Those were six hard months, let me tell you. I never studied so much in my life – after spending the morning doing pushups.

In addition to traffic enforcement I also respond to emergencies in my patrol area. My usual district is home to a number of small towns and a web of state highways. No federal highways, no big cities. When somebody dials 911 in an emergency I may be the nearest responder. Local or county police are also called, but if I'm the first on the scene I have to take charge until the local cops arrive. I like this part of my job because it gives me an opportunity to interact with the people I serve in a positive way. When I respond to a 911 call the people are happy to see me. Nobody likes to get a speeding ticket."

I Am a County Sheriff

"I was a municipal police officer for 20 years before I ran for sheriff. I was always interested in the local political scene and wondered what I could accomplish running the largest law enforcement agency in the county. I knew I wouldn't be a credible candidate until after I had been on the job for a good, long time.

I got started in law enforcement after high school. My first department didn't require a degree to get hired but it did offer a tuition-reimbursement program for officers who wanted to go to college. It was also immediately apparent that advanced education was the key to moving up in the world, as all command-level officers in my department had a bachelor's degree, and some a master's degree. I completed my degree in five years, part time, nights and weekends.

I moved up the ranks quickly. I worked hard and served as a patrol officer, detective, and sergeant. Eventually I entered the command ranks and became a captain. By the time I decided to run for sheriff I was a commander and had built a solid reputation throughout the county. Two decades of hard work paid off when my local political party agreed to back my run for sheriff. I couldn't have done it without their support.

My county is on the edge of a major metropolitan area and is home to more than 500,000 people. About half of the county's residents live in the unincorporated areas that we patrol. The cities are a mix of small and very small, rich and poor. We have every kind of police challenge here.

My main thrust has been to enhance cooperation among departments. My department is the largest single police department in the county. There are a couple of city departments that are also fairly large, but the rest are tiny. I'm no fan of forcing small departments to become subordinate to larger ones. I am convinced that most people prefer to be served by local police who share their commitment to the community. Still, I am a very big fan of solving crimes, so when it comes to murder and organized drug-dealing I am the first person to call for cooperation among the departments.

My proudest achievement was establishing a special task force to go after repeat offenders. The district attorney and I are on the same page about repeat offenders, so we put together a plan to come down as hard as possible on the criminals who commit most of the crimes. The plain truth is that most people convicted of a felony or even a misdemeanor never do it again. They're regular folks who made a bad decision. The overwhelming majority of crime is committed by the same people, over and over again. They slip through the cracks in the criminal justice system and get back on the streets in no time. Now, when we arrest a repeat offender we make sure that doesn't happen. We've reduced crime in the county by almost a third by locking up a handful of people."

I Am a State Police Academy Instructor

"Graduating from military boot camp isn't mandatory to succeed in this position but it sure helps. I graduated from the Marine Corps boot camp many years ago and the lessons I learned there help me to succeed as a police academy instructor today.

I have had a broad and varied career in the state police department. I started out in patrol, as most troopers do, and then did hitches in the capitol police, on the governor's security detail and in investigations.

At the police academy, I teach basic investigative techniques to new recruits from all across the state. I also teach advanced techniques to new detectives. At the recruit level, investigations are fairly simple. We're not expecting new officers to be first-rate detectives any time soon. Most new recruits will become patrol officers when they get back to their departments, and only a handful will become detectives later in their careers. When they do, many of them come back to the academy to delve further into the subject.

Being a detective is a combination of science, logic, and intuition. We use advanced scientific tools to do things like get positive identifications from DNA samples. We use logic to determine motives and whittle down lists of potential suspects. Intuition is what separates good detectives from great detectives. It's a combination of talent and experience that doesn't come together overnight.

I have an associate degree in law enforcement, as do most of my colleagues. I could have earned additional degrees, of course, but policing offers more than enough in-house training programs to keep me busy. I've taken courses at the state academy, some big-city academies, and even Northwestern University, which runs one of the top law enforcement programs in the country. Whether you earn degrees or not, you need to be willing to learn if you want to succeed as a police officer, and even more if you want to succeed as a detective."

I Am a County Marine Patrol Officer

"Most of the time I am a regular county sheriff's deputy serving in patrol, cruising the county looking for signs of trouble, and being ready to respond to emergencies. During the summer I serve on the marine patrol, which is the most fun I've ever had in uniform.

My county is home to a popular recreation area with many small lakes linked together by picturesque channels. Every summer, from Memorial Day to Labor Day, the area explodes with activity. Boats go in the water, restaurants and bars that have been shuttered for the winter open up anew, and people come to the area in droves. Many of them are bound and determined to behave badly. They get in their boats, fill up their coolers, and get the party started. Boating while intoxicated is as dangerous as driving while intoxicated and as illegal. Boating accidents can be horrendous. Even people who aren't hurt by a collision can be thrown into the water. Not everybody can swim, and nobody swims very well when they've been drinking all day. Sometimes people who are unharmed by the crash end up drowning. I do what I can to prevent the crashes.

My team and I patrol the lakes just like we would patrol a city or a highway. We cruise the popular areas, remind people to slow down and observe boat safety, and sometimes we pull people over when we see evidence of a real problem. Most days are basically fun. I chat with the people on the lakes, spend some time in the sun and enjoy myself. People come here to have a good time. Some people cross the line. It's unfortunate, but that's what I'm here for."

PERSONAL QUALIFICATIONS

TO BE A STATE OR COUNTY POLICE officer you need to be scrupulously honest. Police officers not only need to enforce the law but also to uphold it under all circumstances. They need to set the example for everybody else, and they are always under scrutiny. The best police take great pride in staying on the straight and narrow, and encourage those around them to do the same. Nobody notices when regular people get speeding tickets but everybody perks up when a police officer gets caught breaking the law, even for something minor. It is unfortunate but true that there are bad cops who have a habit of "badging" their way out of minor infractions by telling the cops who stop them that they are fellow police officers and should get a free pass. It is even more unfortunate that so many otherwise honest cops let them get away with it. Every once in a while the public finds out, and it makes all cops look bad.

County sheriffs and state troopers need to be absolutely unflappable in their dealings with the public and within their organizations. People who are about to be ticketed or arrested will go to great lengths to avoid their fates. They will try to talk their way out of trouble by appealing to your sentimental side. They may try to bribe you. They may even try to use physical force against you. Police officers do have some latitude in dealing with individual suspects, but once they have started an interaction with a member of the public they must commit to seeing it through to the end. Failure to do so could result in legal consequences for all involved. Police officers should strive to be reasonable and fair in their dealings with the public, but they also have to be firm and resolute.

You must have an unwavering commitment to your mission and your role in the community you serve. State troopers and sheriff's deputies cannot   have "off" days. You are always in the public eye. There are always people counting on you. You do not get to decide which calls you respond to. You also do not get to decide when or where you come face-to-face with danger. If you pursue a career as a deputy sheriff or state trooper you must be able to fully commit, all day, every day.

ATTRACTIVE FEATURES

THE PUBLIC IS FASCINATED BY POLICE. That is definitely an attractive feature of a career in policing. Policing has been defined as the "thin blue line" between order and anarchy. Police officers stand between the vast majority of law-abiding citizens and the few who would do them harm. They also exude an aura of authority that assures the law-abiding, and reminds the law-breaking that they are only one foolish step from serious trouble. The legal and moral mechanisms that make policing work are fascinating, and most people look at police officers with a mixture of respect and trepidation. Respect for their willingness to put themselves in harm's way and trepidation at how they may use their authority – even law-abiding, regular folks sometimes break the speed limit. If you become a state or county police officer the people around you will never look at you the same way again.

The real point of pride in a police career is the opportunity to serve the community. Few professions offer such a visible opportunity to make your community a better place. Sometimes you will feel like you cannot win, as there will always be naysayers who think police are untrustworthy bullies, but mostly you will take great pride in making the community a safer place. Police officers always march in local parades, for example, and they usually get a rousing cheer when they pass by. The police aren't known as "California's Finest" or "Shelby County's Finest" for nothing.

Police officers also take pride in getting bad people off the street. This is the essence of serving the community, but it becomes extra poignant when they actually arrest an offender who has been making life difficult for people. A relatively small number of criminals commit most of the crimes. Anywhere from 10 percent to 20 percent of criminals commit 70 percent to 90 percent of all crimes. These individuals are known as "repeat offenders," and they can become very well known to the police officers in the areas where they commit their crimes. Sentencing laws differ from state to state but in many states repeat offenders can spend relatively little time behind bars, being released in short order for minor crimes so they can commit them again. It is only a matter of time until they do something really stupid that will get them locked up for a long time. Ask a few cops about their proudest moments in uniform. Most of them will tell you that they were never happier than when they finally nabbed a repeat offender they had never quite been able to pin down.

UNATTRACTIVE FEATURES

POLICING CAN BE DANGEROUS. Numbers vary from year to year, but according to statistics compiled by the Federal Bureau of Investigation, about 100 police officers are killed in the line of duty every year in the United States. The two largest causes of death are gunfire and automobile accidents, often during chases. It is true that most American police officers get all the way through their careers without ever firing a weapon in anger or engaging in a truly dangerous high-speed car chase. It is also true, however, that it is a police officer's duty to put him or herself in the line of fire when necessary to protect the community. For every police officer killed in the line of duty there are thousands who suffer serious injuries on the job and thousands more who develop chronic conditions related to decades of police work. Ever wonder why older cops are assigned to safe beats in calm neighborhoods? Because knees, backs and shoulders do not last forever. Twenty years of chasing punks will wear anybody out.

Police departments are government agencies, and subject to politics. When you are a junior deputy or trooper you may be able to ignore most of the politicking, but as you move up in the world, you will have to learn how to negotiate the twists and turns of the institutional machine of which you are a part. Seniority plays a role in who gets the best jobs, as do personal connections. State legislatures and county boards control the funding for police departments. You have read about the budget battles in Congress over funding for the military. One side believes the military should get whatever it needs to complete its mission, while the other side thinks the military takes up too much of the budget and that some of that money should be used on other government programs. State legislatures and county boards have exactly the same arguments over funding for their police departments.

No matter how important your job is, and no matter how much pride you take in it, there will always be people who do not like you. Some people had a bad experience with a grumpy cop during a simple traffic stop, while others suffered through actual police brutality or just have a philosophical problem with cops and what they do. In a country dedicated to freedom and personal liberty, it does not take much to set some people off. Drunk driving checkpoints, for example, have become flashpoints in recent years for those who see American police departments as overstepping their bounds. Cars are stopped at random and the drivers questioned. Many people argue that this is an infringement upon the legal principle of probable cause, in which police need a reason or provocation before they can detain or question somebody. Most courts have decreed that checkpoints can only be used under very limited circumstances, such as on holidays known for excessive drinking.

EDUCATION AND TRAINING

THE TOPIC OF FORMAL EDUCATION for police officers has been the subject of debate for many years. While many argue that policing is the kind of job that can only be learned through experience and on-the-job training, the evolving nature of policing has put a new premium on the skills needed to combat crimes like identity theft.

Historically, cops started their jobs with a high school diploma and a few months of training at a police academy, followed by a year or so in rookie status working alongside a seasoned veteran. Most police academies require between three and six months and are similar to military boot camp. There is a solid argument to be made for this training, as policing is a hands-on profession only some of which can be learned in a classroom. Most police departments still subscribe to this basic approach.

More and more jurisdictions have instituted minimum education requirements for new police officers. The nature of crime has evolved over time, from basic crimes against property and people, to crimes against data and even ideas. The law has also become more complex, with liability becoming an issue in almost everything. The days when most people took orders from cops without hesitation are long gone. Police officers still need the fundamental policing skills they have always needed, but they also need additional abilities.

Your minimum formal education requirement for a career in policing should be an associate degree in law enforcement. A two-year degree has become almost mandatory. Even if the department to which you apply does not have a formal education requirement, you can be sure that many of those you are competing against will possess at least an associate degree. Earning a bachelor's degree will make you even more competitive.

Majoring in law enforcement is the obvious choice, but not the only one. Many police officers have degrees in psychology or sociology because that knowledge is helpful on the street. Others have degrees in business administration and management because they have their sights set on leadership positions.

Not all careerists heading for a career in law enforcement want to wear a uniform. All state police departments and many county sheriff's departments maintain crime labs staffed by civilian employees with degrees in biology, chemistry, engineering, and many other disciplines. Advanced degrees are common in such labs, up to and including doctorates. It is not uncommon for uniformed officers to take off the uniform and slip into civilian jobs, especially after they have put in enough years to earn a pension for their uniformed service.

It should come as no surprise that many police officers are military veterans. All of the armed services train their own police officers, known as military police or masters-at-arms. Any military experience will serve you well if you pursue a career in policing. Police departments are paramilitary organizations, with clear chains of command, uniforms, and many rules delineating their relationship with the civilians they serve. One five-year hitch in the military after high school can give you an advantage over the competition when it comes time to land your first job in law enforcement.

No matter what you decide to major in, you should be sure to take advantage of the opportunity to complete an internship. Many police departments offer internships for aspiring police officers. Most internships are paid and many come with opportunities not extended to regular employees, like special seminars or group discussions with senior leaders. Even if you spend most of your time making coffee, you will have an opportunity to get an inside view of the career you think you want to pursue. You can even walk away after a few months without any penalty. Many careerists get their first real jobs after college with the organizations where they did their internship. Others go back to school and change their major after discovering that their dream career was not really what they wanted.

Whether or not to pursue advanced education is a decision you can put off for a few years. Many police officers earn bachelor's degrees and spend the rest of their careers concentrating on the many training and educational opportunities offered by their departments. Those who aspire to senior leadership positions often earn master's degrees in business administration or public administration.

EARNINGS

EARNINGS FOR STATE AND COUNTY police officers vary widely among different jurisdictions. All state and county police officers are government employees and are paid according to a standard pay scale that applies to all other officers within their department.

Some rural sheriff's departments start new deputies with an annual salary of $35,000, while state police departments in states with a high cost of living may start new hires at $55,000 to $60,000. The wide range of salaries is a reflection of the cost of living in different parts of the United States. Essentially all police departments offer overtime pay for hours worked over 40 hours per week. In fact, some of the highest-paid employees in states and counties are law enforcement officers who make a habit of volunteering for overtime. Overtime is typically 1.5 times the usual hourly rate and may climb to twice the usual rate for working on holidays. Putting in as few as 10 extra hours per week can make a big difference in your paycheck.

Police departments also tend to offer excellent benefits, with the full range of health and dental insurance, paid vacation time, sick days, and paid training days. Most departments also offer defined-benefit pension plans that allow officers to retire with a pension after serving for a certain number of years. Some departments have adopted the military system and allow officers to retire with a 50-percent pension after 20 years of service.

Naturally, pay increases with seniority and responsibility. Most county sheriffs are paid more than $100,000 per year, and many state police chiefs are paid even more. Public pay scales are readily available online. You may have to do a little digging to get to the specifics in a particular jurisdiction.

OPPORTUNITIES

THERE ARE MANY WAYS TO MOVE UP in the world of state and county policing. Military experience will help you land that all-important first job and serve you well later in your career. One hitch in the military after high school or college will go a long way toward getting started with a state or county police department. Police departments are paramilitary organizations that value military experience. You could serve as a military police officer and get real policing experience, but serving in any capacity will help. Many police departments also offer preferential hiring programs for veterans.

Adding credentials to your résumé will always help to advance your career. Police departments offer a wide range of training opportunities, some mandatory and some optional. Take advantage of the optional training. You will expand your horizons, and you may make yourself eligible for future opportunities. Earning a bachelor's degree is probably the surest way to move up in the organization. Some police departments require bachelor's degrees but most do not. Coming into the organization with a four-year degree, or earning one part time after you have been hired, will set you apart from your peers. A master's degree in a subject like public administration or law enforcement will set you up for senior leadership positions in the future.

Every police department has its share of officers who try their best to find low-stress jobs and stay in them. Unlike the military, most police departments do not require uniformed personnel to keep moving up in rank or leave the department. The majority of police officers are troopers or deputies and have no desire to become sergeants – the middle managers – let alone captains or commanders. Dealing with the public is what draws many careerists to policing in the first place. Senior leaders spend most of their time running their departments, as opposed to working with the public. If you want to move into one of these senior positions you can start by volunteering for the hard jobs. Patrol a bad neighborhood. Do a hitch in corrections. Spend a few years on a joint task force with the FBI. Act like you want to move up in the world and you will get you chance.

GETTING STARTED

YOU HAVE YOUR WORK CUT OUT FOR you when the time comes to land your first real job. Be sure you understand the hiring process and have a backup plan if your first choice does not work out. Hiring policies differ from one jurisdiction to the next, but typically require applicants to fill out an application and submit a résumé in order to determine if they have the basic qualifications to become a sheriff's deputy or state trooper. If they do, they are invited to take an exam. Applicants are then usually ranked according to their exam scores. When vacancies open up, the high-scorers are contacted to see if they are still interested in the job. If they are, they are subjected to a physical fitness test, drug test and some kind of interview or oral board. Only after clearing all of these hurdles are they finally offered a job. This process can easily take more than a year. Most aspiring police officers apply to more than one department to better their chances that something will open up sooner or later. You will probably need to get a job to support yourself during this waiting period. Try to get something relevant to your career goals, like working as a security guard.

Studying for the exam is critical to your chances of success. This is especially true if you want to work for a small county sheriff's department. Turnover is very slow in police departments. Careerists who decide they do not like the job as much as they thought they would often quit before they get to the five-year mark. After that, however, very few police officers step down until they are eligible for a pension. A small sheriff's department may only have a dozen or so deputies. You could wait a long time for an opening. Your wait will be longer if you are ranked low on the list of applicants. Doing well on the exam will make a real difference.

Be prepared to look further afield if necessary. You need to be prepared for the possibility that there may not be any jobs available in the state or county in which you would like to work. Low turnover, shrinking law enforcement budgets, and bad timing can keep you from working where you want. Large county and state departments often recruit nationally in order to find the best-qualified people for the job.

ASSOCIATIONS

PERIODICALS

WEBSITES

- **American Association of State Troopers**
  www.statetroopers.org

- **California Highway Patrol**
  www.chp.ca.gov

- **Center for Problem-Oriented Policing**
  www.popcenter.org

- **Chicago Police Department**
  www.chicagopolice.org

- **Cook County Sheriff's Office**
  www.cookcountysheriff.org

- **Discover Criminal Justice**
  www.discovercriminaljustice
  .com

- **Discover Policing**
  www.discoverpolicing.org

- **Federal Bureau of Investigation**
  www.fbi.gov

- **Illinois State Police**
  www.isp.state.il.us

- **Institute for Law Enforcement Education**
  www.patips.net

- **International Association of Chiefs of Police**
  www.theiacp.org

■ **Law Enforcement Education Program**
www.leepusa.com

■ **Law Officer**
www.lawofficer.com

■ **Learning for Life**
www.learningforlife.org

■ **Los Angeles Police Department**
www.lapdonline.org

■ **Major County Sheriffs' Association**
www.mcsheriffs.com

■ **New York Police Department**
www.nyc.gov/html/nypd/html/home/home.shtml

■ **New York State Police**
www.troopers.ny.gov

■ **Officer.com**
www.officer.com

■ **Police Chief**
www.policechiefmagazine.org

■ **Police Foundation**
www.policefoundation.org

■ **Police Magazine**
www.policemag.com

■ **PoliceOne**
www.policeone.com

■ **San Diego County Sheriff's Department**
www.sdsheriff.net

■ **United States Department of Justice**
www.justice.gov

www.ingramcontent.com/pod-product-compliance
Lightning Source LLC
Chambersburg PA
CBHW070800180526
45168CB00004B/1696